Ben, Milly, Don and Kal wanted to dress up.

It was Milly's favourite game.

Mum found some dressing up clothes.

Shared Reading

Page to read **together** to introduce the story.

Ben put on a coat.

"I look like Dad," said Ben.

on coat I

Don put on a dress.

"I look like Mum," said Don.

on dress look

Milly put on a little jumper.

"I look like a baby," said Milly.

like baby jumper

LUNCH

Kal got a rattle.

“I look like a baby too,” said Kal.

I baby look

"Look at us," said Don.

"Dressing up is fun!"

us at look

ESS
BO

"I want to dress up again," said Ben.

"Yippee!" said Kal.

again up I

POP it on!

coat

DRESSING UP

dress

DRESSING UP

jumper

DRESS

baby

DRESSING UP

at

DRESSING UP

on

DRESSING UP

like

DRESSING UP

again

DRESSING UP

look

DRESSING UP

I

DRESSING UP

Developing Language Skills

Use the following techniques to help develop your child's language.

Encourage Naming within a Category

Encourage your child to give examples within a category already present, e.g. clothes.

Prompt your child to develop ideas and expand his vocabulary with questions, e.g.:

"What might be in the Dressing Up Box?"; "Ben is wearing a coat – what else is he wearing?"; "Milly is dressed like a baby – what does a baby wear?"

Encourage your child to think of the range of clothing that might be worn by each person the children are dressing up as, e.g. Dad, Mum, a baby.

Asking Questions

Use the illustrations to help your child to understand the story line. Ask your child simple questions relating to the content of each page and encourage him to explore further possibilities, e.g.:

"What did Ben put on when he dressed up as Dad?"; "Who did Don dress up as?"; "Why did Milly have a rattle?"; "Who else dressed up as a baby?"

Encourage your child to expand his ideas around the topic of dressing up by asking questions, e.g.:

"Who else could the children dress up as?"; "What could you wear if you dressed up as a king, a queen, a clown or a doctor?"; "Who would you like to dress up as?"

The POPS reading programme delivers a core vocabulary on everyday topics your child will need at home and at school. The topic(s) covered by this book are:

Dressing

For further help, please download our free manual for Teachers and Parents at:

www.popsresources.com